This notebook belongs to:

....

Date:

....

Made in the USA
San Bernardino, CA
21 January 2020

63450701R00069